In Touch

Newspapers

Chris Oxlade

www.heinemann.co.uk/library
Visit our website to find out more information about **Heinemann Library** books.

To order:
 Phone ++44 (0)1865 888066
 Send a fax to ++44 (0)1865 314091
 Visit the Heinemann Bookshop at www.heinemann.co.uk/library to browse our catalogue and order online.

First published in Great Britain by Heinemann Library, Halley Court, Jordan Hill, Oxford OX2 8EJ, a division of Reed Educational and Professional Publishing Ltd. Heinemann is a registered trademark of Reed Educational & Professional Publishing Ltd.

OXFORD MELBOURNE AUCKLAND JOHANNESBURG BLANTYRE
GABORONE IBADAN PORTSMOUTH NH (USA) CHICAGO

© Reed Educational and Professional Publishing Ltd 2001
The moral right of the proprietor has been asserted.

Designed by Visual Image
Illustrations by Visual Image
Originated by Ambassador Litho Ltd.
Printed in Hong Kong/China

06 05 04 03 02   06 05 04 03 02
10 9 8 7 6 5 4 3 2 1   10 9 8 7 6 5 4 3 2 1
ISBN 0431 11280 0 (hardback)   ISBN 0431 11287 8 (paperback)

British Library Cataloguing in Publication Data

Oxlade, Chris
  Newspapers. – (In touch)
  1. Newspapers – Juvenile literature
  I. Title
  070.1'72

Acknowledgements

The Publishers would like to thank the following for permission to reproduce photographs: *The Age*: p17; Corbis: pp6, 8, 9, 22, 23, 27, 28, Gail Mooney p13; *Daily Mirror*: p29; Eye Ubiquitous: p25; *Financial Times*: p21; United States Department of Agriculture Animal and Plant Health Inspection Service Legislative and Public Affairs: p17; Impact: p11; *International Herald Tribune*: p26; PA News Photo: pp10, 12; Photodisc: pp4, 5; Raymond Gubbay: p17; Sainsbury's: p17; Sheena Verdun-Taylor: pp15, 18, 20, 24; Stone/Bruce Ayres: p16; Tudor Photography: p14.

Cover photograph reproduced with permission of Trevor Clifford.

Every effort has been made to contact copyright holders of any material reproduced in this book. Any omissions will be rectified in subsequent printings if notice is given to the Publisher.

Contents

Any words appearing in the text in bold, **like this**, are explained in the Glossary.

Communication

Communication lets people in different places talk to each other. It tells us about things that happen in other countries. It entertains us. The six main types of communication are telephone, post, newspapers, television, radio and the **Internet**.

Many people buy a newspaper every day. It helps them to keep up to date with the news.

Stories

Every day, hundreds of millions of people all over the world buy a newspaper. The newspaper stories tell people about things happening in their own countries and in the rest of the world.

This book is about newspapers. It tells you how a daily newspaper is made. It also tells you about the people who work on a newspaper.

This newsagent's shop sells newspapers in different languages. There are thousands of different newspapers around the world.

Newspapers

There are thousands of different newspapers around the world. Most newspapers are daily newspapers, produced every day. There are also weekly and monthly newspapers.

Some newspapers are local newspapers that contain news about a town or city. National newspapers contain news from a whole country.

These Chinese people are reading a newspaper stuck on a notice-board. It is called a wall newspaper. The people read it on the notice-board and do not buy their own copy.

Making a newspaper

Newspaper reporters find news stories and write about them. The stories can be about things like politics, fires, crimes or sport. The written stories are called **copy**.

Photographers take photographs to go with the story. The story and photographs are arranged on the newspaper's pages. There are also **adverts** and the weather forecast. When all the pages are full, the newspaper is printed.

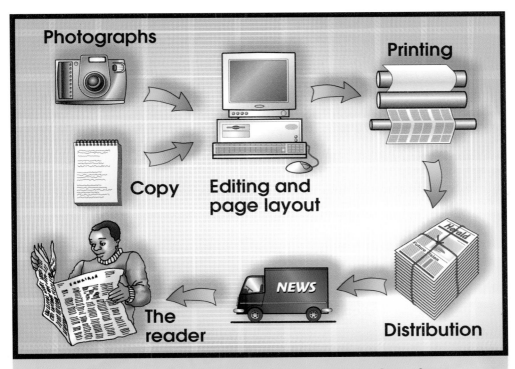

Photographs

Printing

Copy

Editing and page layout

The reader

Distribution

This diagram shows you how a newspaper is written, printed and **distributed**. Many different people have to work hard to get every stage ready on time.

Finding news

Most stories in a newspaper are **investigated** by reporters who work for the newspaper. Some reporters only write stories about one subject, such as sport.

A story

Imagine a factory catches fire. Someone telephones the newspaper. A reporter and a photographer rush to the factory.

These newspaper reporters and photographers are at the scene of an important news event. They may have to wait for hours to get information for their stories.

This newspaper reporter writes down facts about a news event at the scene. She also has a small cassette recorder for recording interviews.

The reporter writes down facts in a notebook to help him or her write the story. He or she asks the factory workers about how the fire started and the fire-fighters how they are fighting the fire. The photographer takes photographs of the burning factory.

News agencies

A **news agency** collects and writes news stories for newspapers. Many newspapers get stories about other countries from news agencies. This is cheaper than having their own reporters all around the world.

Editing stories

The reporter at the factory fire writes the story on a **portable** computer. They then plug the computer into a telephone line. This sends the **copy** to the newspaper.

Choosing stories

A newspaper can have several sections, such as world, sports and business news. Each section may have its own **editor**. The editor looks at the stories that reporters send in and chooses the best ones for the section.

This reporter is using a **satellite** telephone system to send a report and photographs from the Himalaya Mountains in Nepal to his office in London.

Foreign Desk

Here, newspaper **journalists** are working in their newspaper's offices. They may have to work very long hours to report on an important story.

The stories that the editors choose are given to people called **sub-editors**. They make sure that the story makes sense, and that all the words are spelled correctly. They also cut out or add words so that the copy fits the newspaper page.

The Editor-in-chief is in charge of the whole newspaper. They meet with the other editors every day to decide which stories to put on the front page.

Newspaper pictures

Editors always want a good photograph for the newspaper's front page. A good photograph can sometimes tell a story better than words. It shows the scene or the people involved.

Some stories have maps and graphs instead of photographs. These are usually drawn on a computer.

This newspaper photographer is looking at his pictures on a computer. He sends the best ones to the newspaper office.

Digital photographs

Most newspaper photographers use **digital cameras**. A photographer takes photographs and puts them on to a computer. They look at the screen and pick the best photographs.

The photographer then plugs the computer into a telephone line and sends the photographs to the newspaper office. The picture editor chooses the best photograph to go with the story.

Choosing a part of a photograph to print is called cropping. The white boxes on this photograph show two crops that would make good pictures.

Newspaper design

Every newspaper looks different. The newspaper's name at the top of the front page is very important. It is printed large so that people can easily see it.

Stories in columns

There are narrow strips of words called columns on each page of a newspaper. The news stories go down the columns.

Different people like different newspapers. Some newspapers look more exciting or interesting than others.

Making up the pages

Editors work out how to fit the stories on to a newspaper's pages. They use a small plan of each page. On the plan they mark where each story and picture goes.

The plans are then stored on a computer. **Sub-editors** and **designers** put the words and pictures on the pages. The computer automatically puts the words into columns.

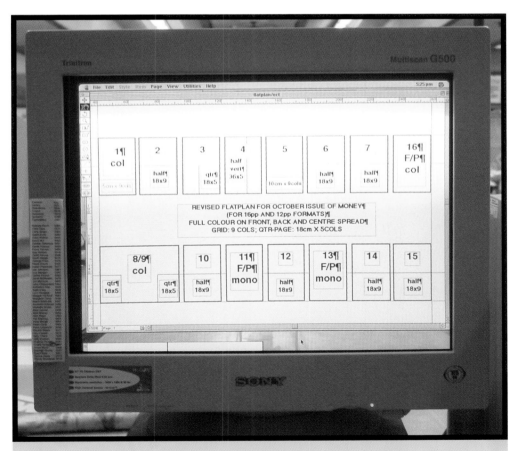

This is a newspaper plan on a computer screen. It shows what will go on each page.

Advertising

Newspaper companies get some money from selling newspapers, but they get more from advertising. Up to half the space in some newspapers is taken up by **adverts**.

Anybody who puts an advert in a newspaper has to pay. The bigger the advert is, the more they have to pay. A whole page advert in a national newspaper is very expensive!

These people work in the advertising department of a newspaper company. People ring up and pay the company to have their advert appear in the newspaper.

Display and classified adverts

Display adverts are large adverts and can take half a page or a whole page of a newspaper.

Readers can put their own small adverts in a newspaper. These are called classified adverts. They appear under headings like 'Cars for Sale' or 'Houses for Rent'. Local newspapers can often contain hundreds of classified adverts.

Display adverts often contain pictures to attract readers. Classified adverts don't need to be so eye-catching.

Ready to print

A newspaper page is finished when all the stories, pictures and **adverts** have been put on the page on the computer.

Making a plate

The computer sends information about the page to a machine. The machine makes a metal **printing plate** for each page. On the plate there is a pattern of the letters and pictures on the page.

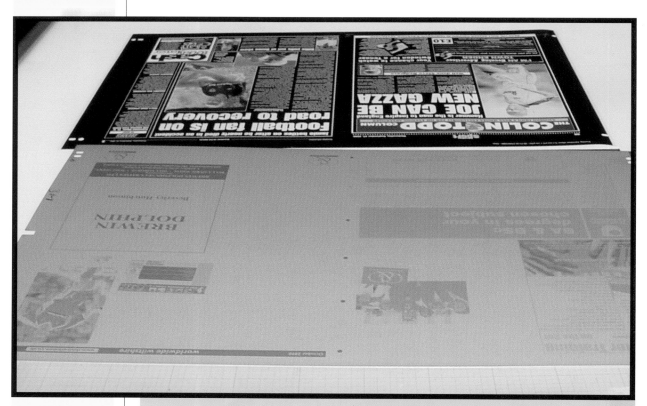

At the bottom you can see a printing plate. It was made by laying film (which you can see at the top) over the plate and exposing it to light.

Last-minute changes

A daily newspaper is printed the evening before the newspaper is sold. For example, the newspaper that you read on Friday is printed on Thursday evening.

Most of the printing plates are ready by the middle of evening. But some pages still have gaps. These are filled by stories that arrive late in the evening. They might be reports on soccer matches or films, for example.

When the final stories are ready they are put into the gaps. Then the plates for the last pages are made.

Newspapers print photographs as groups of tiny dots. In this magnified photograph you can see that the larger dots make up the darker areas.

Printing

Newspapers are printed by huge printing machines called **presses**. Inside a press the metal **printing plates** for the pages are wrapped around big cylinders.

Inky rollers

Next to each cylinder there is an inky roller. The cylinder and the roller spin round. The roller puts ink on to the printing plate. The ink then goes on to a rubber cylinder, which prints the words and pictures on the paper.

This photograph shows a cylinder wrapped in plates spinning around.

Colours

Both black and coloured inks are used to print newspapers. There are three colours of coloured inks. They are cyan (blue), magenta (red) and yellow. Only some pages have colour on them, most are black and white.

These pages have already been through the printing press. They will now be cut and folded into finished newspapers.

Paper and printing

We call the paper used for newspapers 'newsprint'. A newspaper **press** uses up to 50 massive rolls of newsprint every day. Each roll weighs a tonne. If one was completely unrolled, it would be about 15 kilometres long!

The rolls spin round very fast and the end of the paper whizzes into the press. Each roll only lasts about 20 minutes. Before it runs out, the printers get a new roll ready to replace it.

Here you can see huge rolls of newsprint in a paper-making factory. A robot truck is moving a roll.

Printing the pages

Some pages in newspapers are printed in black and some are printed in colour. The black and colour pages are printed on different rollers. The pages are then automatically collected together.

A newspaper printing press can produce 70,000 newspapers every hour! Each newspaper takes just a few seconds to print. National newspapers print millions of copies every day.

A print worker checks that a finished newspaper has been printed properly.

To the shops

Long **conveyor belts** carry the finished newspapers from the printing **press** to a **distribution** area. Machines stack the newspapers into piles of 50 or 100.

The machines tie the piles into neat bundles. Another machine sticks a label on each bundle. The label shows the town or city the bundle is going to. The bundles go along another conveyor belt and are then loaded on to trucks.

These bundling machines work fast to keep up with the printing press, so that the newspapers get out to the shops on time.

Finished newspapers are loaded into a truck. They will be driven to distribution centres, shops and news stands.

The trucks drive to distribution centres. There, the newspapers are loaded into vans and delivered to shops and **news stands**. It is only twelve hours since the reporters wrote their stories.

National newspapers are printed in two or three different towns or cities. This means the trucks do not have to go too far. It makes it quicker to get the newspapers to the shops.

Internet news

Most large newspapers have **Internet websites**. The newspaper's stories appear on the website. It can have photographs, sounds and video too.

If a big news event happens early in the day, the story only appears in a newspaper the next day. But a story can be put on the website as soon as the reporter writes it.

This is a web page from a newspaper on the Internet. New stories can appear on a website almost as soon as they happen.

Newspapers anywhere

Already people can use televisions, **palm-top** computers and mobile phones to look up information on the Internet. This will make reading newspapers on the Internet more popular.

People who have difficulty seeing can use newspapers in Braille and speaking newspapers on cassettes.

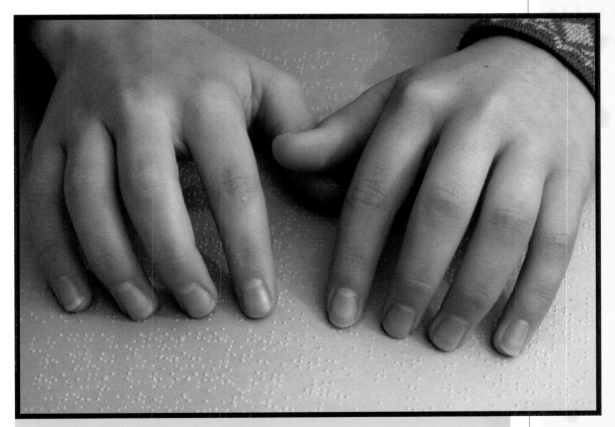

Braille is a collection of raised bumps on the page. For each letter, the bumps are arranged differently. Many newspapers have **editions** printed in Braille for the blind.

Newspaper times

Here are some important events in the history of newspapers.

1st century AD People living in Ancient Rome have a simple newspaper which is stuck on a wall.

1440s In Germany, Johannes Gutenburg builds the first printing **press**. Before this, people had to write books by hand.

1600s People make the first proper newspapers in northern Europe.

These print workers in New York in 1909 are making pages with metal **type**. This will be used to print a newspaper. Computers now do this job.

This newspaper image shows text including the masthead "THE DAILY MIRROR" dated "April 16, 1912" with headlines such as "WORLD'S GREATEST LINER AT THE BOTTOM OF THE ATLANTIC AFTER COLLIDING WITH AN ICEBERG" and "'MANY LIVES LOST' IN DISASTER TO TITANIC."

This **edition** of the *Daily Mirror* was published on the day the famous passenger ship *Titanic* sank in the Atlantic Ocean.

1690 The first American newspaper is **published** in Boston.

1851 Paul Reuter starts the first **news agency** in London.

1903 The *Daily Mirror* is published for the first time. It is the first tabloid (half-sized newspaper).

1970s/1980s Computers begin to be used to make newspapers.

1998 People can look at newspapers on the **Internet** for the first time.

Glossary

advert words and pictures that tell people about things that are for sale, such as cars and houses

conveyor belt moving band which carries things from one place to another

copy the words in a newspaper story

designer person who decides how a newspaper will look

digital camera camera that takes photographs electronically and stores them in computer memory. It does not need film.

distribution sending parcels or packages from one place to many places

edition one version of a newspaper

editor person who chooses stories or pictures for a newspaper

Internet huge network of computers that stretches right around the world

investigate find out about something

journalist person who finds out and writes about the news

news agency company that writes news stories and sells them to newspapers

news stand small shop where you can buy newspapers

palm-top small computer that you can hold in one hand

portable something that you can easily carry around

press machine that puts patterns of ink on to paper

printing plate flat metal plate in a printing press. It collects ink and passes it on to the paper.

published something printed or put on a website so people can read it

satellite machine in space that goes round the Earth

sub-editor person who checks all the words in a newspaper story to make sure they are correct and that the story is the right length

type letters and numbers that make up stories on the page of a newspaper

website collection of information about a particular subject stored on the Internet

Index